MATH PIRATES

MAKING A SAIL FOR A PIRATE SHIP

A LITTLE BOOK OF **BIG** CHOICES

MATH PIRATES

MAKING A SAIL FOR A PIRATE SHIP

Book 2: Estimation, Area & Beginning Geometry

S.E. BURR

emtippettsbookdesigns.com

OTHER LITTLE BOOKS OF **BIG** CHOICES

Math Pirates: The Complete Quest for the Pickled Pearl
(includes the story inthis current book you're holding
and four others)

Merfriends: The Complete Water Safety Collection

Mage Academy: The Complete Collection

The Adventures of Billy the Chimera Hunter

The Pippa the Werefox Mysteries Volume I
The Pippa the Werefox Mysteries Volume II
The Pippa the Werefox Mysteries Volume III

Learn more about us and get
free ebooks at littlebooksofbigchoices.com

MAKING A SAIL FOR A PIRATE SHIP

When you arrive at the dock, you see many large and impressive ships. It takes you a while to find the Barnacle Bucket, and when you do, you're a little disappointed. It clearly needs some help to be seaworthy. A couple pirates are hard at work with wood and tar patching holes in the sides. Also, the ship is missing one of its sails.

One of the pirates, a bald man with big muscles, sees you watching and waves. It's Uncle Six. He's called Six because he's exactly six feet tall. You wave back and with a speed and grace surprising for his size, he swings out on a long rope, lets go, does a somersault in the air, and then lands beside you on the dock. "You made it!"

You smile. "I made it."

"Great!" he says. "The next thing you need to do in Grandpa Pirate's quest is to get this old ship ready to sail."

"All right," you say. "Should I get some tar and help patch holes?"

"Not this time," he answers. "What we need you to do is get us a sail."

"A sail?" you say.

"A sail," he answers.

You think for a minute. You want to

seem smart and like you know what to do, but you really have no idea. "How?" you ask.

He hands you a small bag of coins. You weigh it in your hand, estimating how much gold it holds, but you're not great at estimating, so you loosen the strings and look inside. "This doesn't seem like very much gold to buy a whole sail with," you say.

He nods sympathetically. "And the more of that you spend, the less money you'll have for provisions for our voyage."

Your eyes widen. "This is for a sail and for provisions?"

He pats you on the shoulder. "A pirate quest is never easy, son."

"Okay…" you say.

He leans closer. "I'll give you a word of advice," he whispers.

"Please do," you whisper back.

"Buying a new sail will cost a lot," he says. "You'll save a lot of money if you sew it yourself."

You almost groan, but stop yourself. You hate sewing. "Okay," you say again. "Thanks, Uncle Six."

"You're welcome," he says and turns toward the gangplank.

"Wait!" you call after him. "What size sail do I need?"

"Sorry, son," Uncle Six answers. "You'll just have to figure that out for yourself." Then he springs up the gangplank and back onto the ship.

You stand on the dock for a minute thinking about what you should do. How will you know what size sail you need? Do you run home and get your aunt's measuring tape? If you did that, you'd have to climb up the mast to measure. You can do that, but it might take a lot of time, and you want to buy the fabric for the sail before the shops close.

You don't need to know the exact size. Like on all ships, this one has a range of sail sizes between the maximum (biggest) and minimum (smallest) sails that would work. You can estimate the size. As you stand there, you realize that Uncle Six is standing right next to the mast with the missing sail. Uncle Six is a hard worker. He doesn't usually just stand around, so what's he doing?

And then it occurs to you! You pull the pencil Grandpa Pirate gave you from your pocket and hold it up in front of your face. Since Uncle Six is far away and the pencil is up close, he looks like he's the same height as the pencil. You measure the mast from this perspective and see that it looks like it's three pencil lengths. That means that it's about 18 feet high because Uncle Six is six feet tall and three times six is 18.

Seeing that you've figured out what he's up to, Uncle Six yawns dramatically and lays down beneath the missing sail's boom. You smile and measure the boom using your pencil and find that it's a little over one and a half Uncle Sixes, meaning it's about 10 feet. So now you know that the sail's luff (height) is about 18 feet and the sail's foot (bottom edge) is about 10 feet. You've got the measurements you need. You turn and walk back up the dock toward Pirate Town.

You need to decide where to buy the fabric, and the way you see it, you have two choices.

The cheapest place for you to find the fabric you need is likely to be the Flotsam

Flea Market. The problem is that you never know what you'll find at the flea market, and you might not find the best sailcloth there. You may have to piece your sail together from used clothes. That sort of patchwork sail would require a lot of time sewing, and likely wouldn't be as good as a sail made from bigger sheets of sailcloth. On the other hand, you may find just what you're looking for and save a lot of money.

Your other option is to buy the fabric at Fortune Fabrics. The fabric for sale at that shop is expensive. However, you're almost certain to find sailcloth there that will be easy to sew and will make a strong, lightweight sail.

So what do you do?

Do you go to Flotsam Flea Market (turn to page 10)?

or

Do you go to Fortune Fabrics (turn to page 21)?

You're back on the dock, and Uncle Six has given you money to buy fabric for a sail. This time you're going to make a different choice and head to Flotsam Flea Market.

THE FLOTSAM FLEA MARKET

The Flotsam Flea market is an open-air market made up of a bunch of cobbled together stalls of all sizes and shapes. You can buy pirate plunder of all sorts, and if you take the time to hunt through it all, you can get some great bargains.

As you walk into the market an array of smells hits your nose: frying fish, herbs and spices, the dung of horses and sheep, hay, and a thousand other smells that you can't identify but that fill you with excitement. The Flotsam Market is always fun.

As you wander between the stalls, you see many wonderful things, and you wish you could spend the money in your pouch how you like instead of saving it for a sail and provisions. But maybe this itself is a test. A true captain puts the needs of the ship first. But there are so many temptations!

One booth sells nothing but toys. There are ball and cup games, tops painted in bright colors, and stick ponies. The ponies' heads are carved and painted so realistically that you expect them to neigh and nip at you as you walk by.

A clothes seller has many, many striped shirts. You love striped shirts. They're so fashionable! You would look like such a dashing pirate captain if you had one! Oh well. You stop at the clothes seller, though, to see if he has anything that could be sewn together to make a sail. Imagine a sail made of a patchwork of striped shirts! But you know that that would take too long to sew, and the shirts cost too much to be used that way, anyway.

Movement above catches your eye and you glimpse the bright feathers of a flying parrot. You make eye contact with the bird. It's looking right at you! Lots of Pirates have parrots. They're not rare in Pirate Town, but this one looks an awful lot like Pamela the Parrot, the pet of Percival the sneaky Pirate. Percival and Pamela are a very tricky duo, and you know they would do anything to get your treasure map and the treasure it leads to.

You don't see Percival, but if Pamela's

here, he probably is too. He's probably hiding nearby and watching you. You need to lose them, so you cut through a stall selling fish pies and out the back. Then you hurry, weaving this way and that between stalls. You cut through another stall, this one selling designer eye patches. "Hey what do you think you're doing?" the seller calls out as you hurry by.

"Sorry," you say and keep going.

You think you must have lost Percival and the parrot, so you stop to catch your breath, and you see something really interesting at the front of a stall. A ship inside a bottle! It's a small model ship, sure, but it's still way too big to have fit through the opening in the bottle. "How on earth did they get it in there?" you ask.

The seller laughs. "That's a mystery," he says, and then turns back to another customer.

"Maybe they built it inside there,"

whispers a girl standing next to you. She has long brown hair in two braids, and she's wearing a great striped shirt.

"No way," you answer. "They couldn't get their hands inside the bottle to build it."

"Maybe they have special, long, thin tools they used to build it inside there," she says.

"Oh!" you say, "maybe so."

"Or," she goes on, "maybe they have little hinges at the bottom of the masts and they put the ship into the bottle with the masts all folded down so it'll fit through the bottleneck. Then, when they get it in there, they use a string to pull the masts up."

"Oh my! You may be right. You're really smart," you tell her. She may even be as smart as your friend Marina.

"Thanks," she says. "I'm Becky."

"I'm Patrick," you answer.

Just then, the parrot you saw earlier swoops down and lands on Becky's shoulder.

"Oh, no!" you say.

"What?" she asks.

"Is that Pamela?" you ask. "Do you know Percival the Pirate?"

"Who?" she asks and then she says, "No, this is just my parrot, Polly."

"Polly?" you ask.

"Polly," she answers.

"That's a relief," you say and wipe your forehead. You were starting to sweat.

"What are you looking for at the market?" she asks.

"Cloth for a sail," you answer, "but I'm not having much luck."

She smiles. "Your luck has just turned."

"What?" you ask.

"Follow me," she says. "I know just the

thing."

You follow her to a stand at the edge of the market. It sells dishes, silverware, and best of all, used tablecloths. "What size do you need?" she asks.

"The mast is 18 feet, and the boom is ten feet," you say.

"We should take off two feet in both directions to make sure it's not too big," she says.

"Right," you agree.

She rummages through a crate sitting on the ground, and pulls out a stack of matching white tablecloths, which are heavily stained with food. They have a note pinned to them telling their size and price. They're square, eight feet by eight feet, and the price is very reasonable.

"Can we lay these out on the beach to see how they'll fit?" Becky asks the seller and gestures to the beach beyond his stall.

He shrugs. "Sure. Not like they can get much dirtier."

Becky and you lay out two tablecloths on the beach. "There," she says. "That's your rectangular sail: 16 by eight."

"It's a triangular sail," you tell her.

She smiles and pulls a long string from her pocket. "Hold that at the corner," she says.

You do, and she hands you one end of the string and then goes to the corner diagonally across from you and pulls the string tight so it makes a line, cutting the rectangle into two triangles. Or two triangular sails! "An eight by eight tablecloth is 64 square feet. Once you cut it and piece it together, you'll only need one of these tablecloths to make your sail."

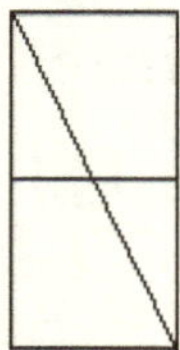

"That's great!" you say.

"Who's going to sew it?" she asks.

You shrug. "I will. I can sew and I'll ask my aunt to help." You CAN sew, but you're not very good at it, and your aunt isn't either, but you're sure she'll help if you ask her.

"You could do that..." she says, "or..."

"Or what?" you ask.

"I'll help you," she says. "I'm a great sewer. I have the second fastest needle in Pirate

Town. I'll have your sail done in no time, and all it'll cost you is a second tablecloth."

"You want a tablecloth?" you ask.

She nods. "I need a new sail, too. What do you say?"

You stop and think. Should you buy a second tablecloth for Becky so she'll help you sew the sail? This will undoubtedly save time. It'll cost you more, but the tablecloths are pretty cheap. You think you can afford it with enough money left over for provisions.

Or will you ask your aunt to help you? This is free, but will take longer and you might mess it up. Neither of you are very good at sewing.

Ask Becky for help (turn to page 32).

or

Ask your aunt for help (turn to page 42).

You're back on the dock, and Uncle Six has given you money to buy fabric for a sail. This time you're going to make a different choice and head to Fortune Fabrics.

FORTUNE FABRICS

You walk into Fortune Fabrics, Pirate Town's only fabric shop, and you can't help but be excited by all the stripes you see—brown stripes, red stripes, blue stripes, black stripes, gold stripes. You're a pirate who likes to be fashionable, and what's more fashionable than stripes? Striped shirts, striped pants, striped hats—you love them all. You would even wear striped shoes if they made them. They don't, but maybe they should. What an exciting idea! You could paint stripes onto the leather!

You close your eyes, blocking out all the beautiful stripes, and take a deep breath. This is no time to get distracted. You're here for a sail and unfortunately sailcloth isn't striped.

But why is that?

Wouldn't that look great?

A fashionable sail for a fashionable pirate?

You shake your head and take another deep breath. You need to make a sail quickly and cheaply. That means no stripes.

Opening your eyes, you see the shop keeper looking at you. She is wearing lots of stripes, and lots of gold and pearls, too. She looks fashionable and rich, which doesn't bode well for you getting a good deal. Clearly she makes big profits selling fabric.

"Are you well, young man?" she asks.

"Yes, quite well," you answer, "just a bit overwhelmed with all the stripes."

She laughs. "Yes. Yes! I sell some wonderful stripes. My name is Madame Dubois. How can I help you?"

"I need fabric to make a sail," you say.

"Excellent!" she replies. "You've come to the right place." She pulls a bolt of white fabric from the shelf and partly unrolls it. "Feel this," she says.

You do.

Madame Dubois goes on. "This here is premium sailcloth, nothing stronger or lighter. You can sail a galleon with this. Nice, isn't it?"

You nod. "Very nice, but I don't need a sail for a galleon. I just need a sail for a small schooner."

"Just because your ship is small doesn't mean it's not special," says Madame Dubois. "Quality cloth means quality sailing. Make your sail from this and you'll be amazed by how fast and nimble your little boat can be."

Nimble isn't the first word that comes to mind when you think of the Barnacle Bucket, but maybe it could be. Perhaps she's right. On the other hand, the sack of coins your uncle gave you is very light. If you buy that you won't have money for provisions and you'll starve on your way to find the treasure. "I don't have much money," you tell her. "I need inexpensive cloth."

Just then the bell on the door jingles behind you, and the shopkeeper gives a wide smile. "Captain Martin!" she calls.

"Just have a look around," she says to you

as she walks away.

You look around, but do not know where to start.

"Psst, lad," someone says, and you think of that sneaky pirate, Percival and his parrot Pamela.

You see the person talking to you and it's not Percival or Pamela. It's another pirate, a friendly looking female pirate sitting at a table near the back of the shop. "Aye?" you say.

She beckons you closer.

You see several other pirates seated at the table with her, all sewing. This must be a pirate sewing circle. You aren't surprised. Grandpa Pirate's first mate, Pirate Pete, is in a pirate crochet circle. Pirates can have all different kinds of hobbies.

The pirate lady says, "The discount fabric is over there," and she points to a rack. "What you want is that one on the bottom left."

You look at the price pinned to the bolt, and she's right. It's much more affordable than the fabric that Madame Dubois showed you. However, it's not a full bolt. "Will there be enough?" you ask.

"How much do you need?" the pirate asks.

You blush. "I'm not sure," you say.

"Do you have the measurements of the mast and the boom?" she asks.

You nod. "The mast is about 18 feet and the boom is 10."

"All right," she says and pulls out a scrap of paper. "Anyone got a pencil?"

You take your pencil from your pocket and hand it to her.

"You don't want your sail to be too big," she says, "and it doesn't have to keep the same proportions." She taps her chin with the pencil. "We'll take two feet off each side. That way it won't be too big and it won't be too small either."

She draws a rectangle on the paper and marks the tall side 16 and the bottom side 8.

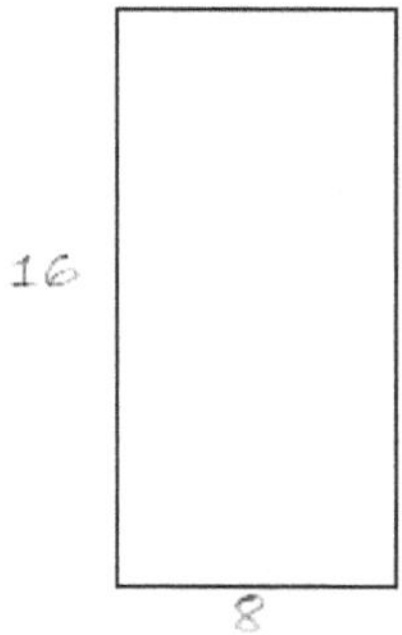

"To know how many square feet of fabric you need, you can draw squares—16 by 8." She draws lines in the rectangle to make a bunch of squares. "If you count the squares you'll know how many square feet you need," she says.

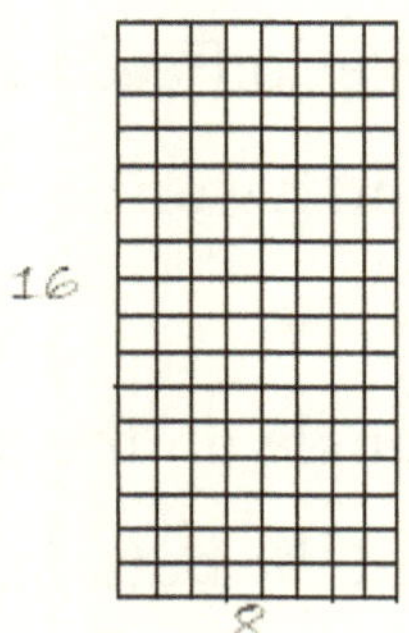

You start to count.

She interrupts you, "Or you can just multiply the height by the width. 16 times eight equals 128 square feet of fabric for a rectangular sail with those dimensions." She eyes the fabric bolt. "You may not have enough."

"It's a triangular sail," you tell her.

"Oh good," she says, and draws a diagonal line from the top left to the bottom right of the rectangle. Now her drawing looks like two identical sails, one right side up and one upside down. "A triangular sail with those measurements will take half as much fabric as a rectangular one. One hundred twenty-eight square feet divided by two means you'll need 64 square feet for your sail." She looks again at the bolt of fabric. "That's plenty," she says. "I think you've found your sailcloth."

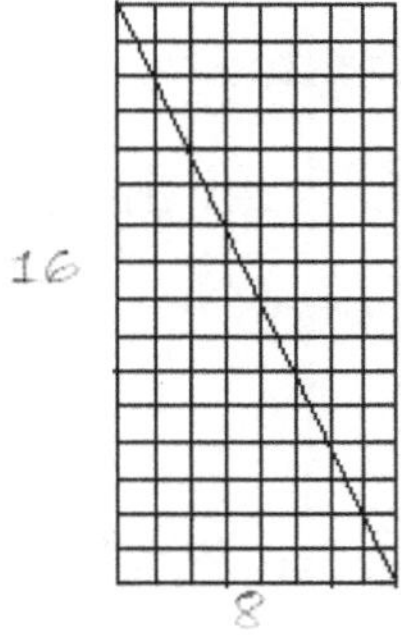

You smile. "Thank you so much!"

She smiles back. "Do you need help sewing your sail? Our circle was just saying that it's been a while since we had a big project to work on together. We'd be happy to help you with it."

"I'm happy to help, too," says Madame Dubois, walking up. Her other customer has left. "In addition to selling fabric I offer my services as a seamstress, and I've got the fastest needle in Pirate Town. Hire me and you'll have your sail ready in half the time it'll take if you work with these amateurs."

"That's true," said the pirate, "if you can pay for it. What do you want to do?"

Do you ask the sewing circle to help you make the sail (turn to page 52)?

or

Do you hire Madame Dubois (turn to page 59)?

You're back on the beach with Becky, and this time you're going to make a different choice and ask her to help you make the sail.

ASK BECKY FOR HELP

You decide to ask Becky to help you sew the sail.

It'll cost you a little more to buy the second tablecloth, but you saved so much money by shopping at the Flotsam Flea Market that you can afford it. Your only other idea is to ask your aunt to help you, and she's not very good at sewing. It would take the two of you a long time and you might mess it up. This way you think it'll be done fast and it'll be done right.

"Where should we go to sew it?" you ask.

She shrugs. "Why not right here?"

"Here?" You ask, surprised. "Outside on the beach?"

"Exactly," she answers. "The tide doesn't reach here. We won't get the fabric wet, or get it washed out to sea or anything."

"I know," you say, feeling embarrassed. You're not sure why you're so surprised by the idea of outdoor sewing. "It's just that I've only ever seen people sew indoors."

"Anything you can do inside is more fun outside," she says.

"Anything?" you ask.

She laughs. "Maybe not anything, but most things, and definitely sewing."

"The sail might blow away," you say.

She licks her finger and holds it up, testing the wind. "Maybe in a storm, but not in this gentle breeze."

"Hmm." You think about it for a moment. "All right. Let's do it here."

"Great," she answers. "Now go pay the seller."

You do, and then Becky and you get to work making your sail.

She folds the tablecloth in half and uses your pencil to mark the center of the top edge where the fold is. Then she lays it back out flat and draws a straight line between the mark and the corner of the tablecloth.

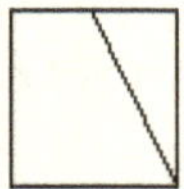

She pulls a pair of scissors from her pocket. Polly, who has been hopping around and digging at the sand with her beak, says "Pretty!" and makes a move toward the scissors.

"Don't even think about it," says Becky. The bird gives her a long, offended stare and then goes back to digging in the sand.

Becky cuts along the line she drew. "Polly likes shiny things."

"Gold!" Polly squawks.

Becky starts sewing the piece she cut onto the top edge of the other piece.

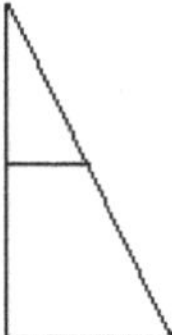

"What do I do?" you ask.

"Do the same thing I just did to the other

tablecloth," she answers. "That one's yours."

"That one's mine?" you ask. "I thought this one was mine."

She shakes her head. "I'm making my sail first."

"Oh," is all you say.

"Don't worry," she tells you. "I'll have both sails done in less time than it would have taken you to make one."

She's probably right. You carefully copy the steps she took on the first tablecloth. You ask her to check your line before you cut it.

She tells you it's fine. The line you cut isn't completely straight, but you take your time and do your best.

Finishing the seam on her sail, she looks at yours. "Good enough," she says and starts to sew it.

Both sails are quickly finished. Becky

stands. "Come on, Polly!" she says.

The bird ignores her.

She whistles. Nothing. "Polly!" Still nothing.

You grow suspicious. "Pamela!" you say, and the bird squawks and looks your way.

Becky chuckles. "You caught me," she says, and then, "Pamela, come!"

The bird flies up and perches on her shoulder.

"I knew I recognized her!" you say.

"Yep," she says. "Percival the Pirate is my papa."

"That sneaky pirate is your papa!" you say.

"Yep," she says, "I'm his daughter."

You look at the new sail she's holding.

"Are you going to take my sail from me after I helped you make yours?" she asks.

"No," you say, frowning. "You earned it fair and square."

"Good," she says. "Thanks for the fabric. We needed to get our boat in good working order to go after that treasure."

"What treasure?" you ask.

She winks. "That one you've got a map for."

"What!" you say, shocked. "How do you know where it is?"

"I don't," she answers, "but you do."

"And you're planning to follow me," you say, "and I helped you get the sail you need to do it."

She shrugs. "Don't feel bad," she says. "If you hadn't bought me the fabric, I would have gotten a new sail one way or another."

She turns and starts walking away. She looks back. "I'll see you soon," she says.

A chill runs down your back. You got your sail quickly and cheaply, but you're in trouble. Becky, Percival's daughter, is sneaky just like he is.

Your decisions here worked out well. You got the fabric you needed cheaply, and you have a good working sail, though it's dirty. Becky tricked you, but there was no harm done. You're sure that she would have gotten the sail she needed, with or without you. You have plenty of money left for provisions, but you'll look for good deals, anyway. Pirates should be thrifty, after all.

You successfully completed this step in your quest. You're worried about what Percival and Becky are up to, so you'll keep a careful eye out for them as you continue your quest and set sail to find the treasure.

This book has four different endings so if you haven't seen them all, you can:

Go back one step and ask your aunt to help you make the sail (turn to page 41).
Go back two steps and go to Fortune Fabrics rather than Flotsam Flea Market
(turn to page 20).
Go back to the beginning and re-read the first scene (turn to page 1).
Or if you've read all four endings,
turn to page 63.

You're back on the beach with Becky, and this time you're going to make a different choice and ask your aunt for help making the sail.

ASK YOUR AUNT
FOR HELP

"Thank you for helping me find a good deal on fabric and for helping me figure out how much I need," you say to Becky. You pause. You feel a little guilty, because she's helped you a lot, but you need to save as much money as you can for provisions. Besides, you're a little suspicious. Her parrot, Polly, looks an awful lot like Pamela, Percival's parrot. You go on. "I'm going to ask my aunt to help me sew the sail. I need to save as much money as I can."

Becky grimaces. She looks mad, but then she shrugs and smiles. "All right," she says. "I'll get the sail I need another way."

You nod and turn away. "See you around," you call.

"See you!" says Becky.

"See you!" squawks the parrot.

You pay for the tablecloth and head to your aunt's house.

It's a nice little place that she maintains herself. She's good with her hands. The house has a great garden full of vegetables, fruits, and lots of flowers. That's where you find your aunt.

"You want me to help you sew your sail?" she asks, standing and brushing her dirty hands on her apron. "You know I'm bad at sewing, right?"

You nod. "I'm bad at it, too."

Aunt Penny laughs. "Then shouldn't you ask someone for help who knows what they're doing?"

"I need to save as much money as I can for provisions," you tell her.

She nods. Your aunt has powerful feelings about properly provisioned ships. "All right," she says. "Let's give it a try."

You lay the tablecloth flat on the floor of the kitchen.

"How do we turn this square cloth into a triangular sail?" Aunt Penny asks.

"Hmm." You remember how Becky used a string to mark a diagonal line from one corner of the rectangle she laid out to the other. You do the same with the square and draw a line from one corner to another. Then you cut it.

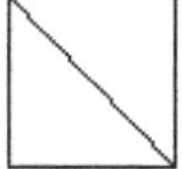

"Now what?" Aunt Penny asks. "How do the pieces go together?"

You try a few arrangements, but it's hopeless. They don't fit. You have two triangular sails, both half as big as you need. You've made a mistake.

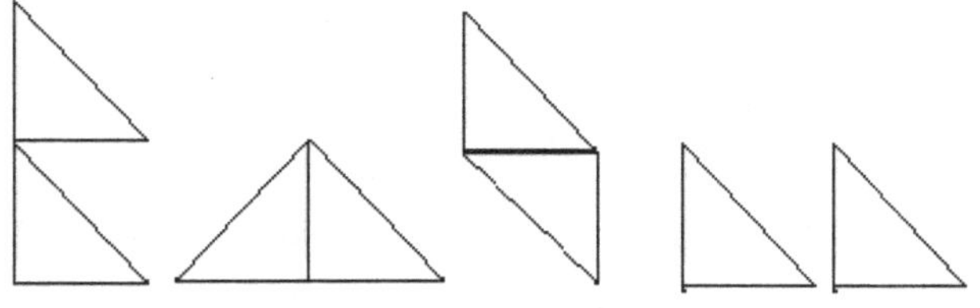

"Let's sit down with a piece of paper and figure this out," your aunt says. Drawing on the paper, you work out that the cut should have gone from the center of the top edge to the bottom corner.

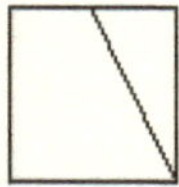

"Maybe we can sew the pieces back together and cut again?" you ask.

"We could..." she says. "But it'll take a long time since we're not very good sewers. Could you get another tablecloth?"

You nod. "Yes. They're not very expensive. I'll go get another."

You go back to the booth where you bought the first tablecloth and try to buy another one, but the seller gives you a price that is double what you paid before. You ask him why.

"That's the price for two," he says. "The one you're buying now and the one your friend took."

"My friend?" you ask.

"Becky," he answers. "She said you'd pay for it when you came back."

"What!" you exclaim. "I told her I wouldn't buy one for her!"

"That's not what she said," says the man. "Was she lying?"

"Yes!" you answer.

The man makes a tutting sound. "That girl is as sneaky as her father."

"Who's her father?" you ask.

"Percival the Pirate," he answers. "Didn't you recognize the parrot?"

You don't know what to say. You did recognize it, but she said its name was Polly. You feel very foolish for being tricked. That's one sneaky girl. You take a deep breath. "I didn't tell her I'd pay for hers. Can I just have this one at the regular price?"

He shakes his head. "Sorry. You want it, you'll have to pay for both."

Grumbling, you pull the money from your pouch and pay for two tablecloths. Now you've bought three when you should have only needed one. You got a good price for them so you should still have enough money for provisions but you'll have to be thrifty. It takes you and your aunt quite a bit of time to do the sewing, but you finish eventually.

Your decisions here had mixed results. You bought three tablecloths when you only needed one. This was both because of Becky's trickery, and because you didn't know what you were doing and messed up your first attempt at making a sail. You got a working sail in the end, though it's dirty, inexpertly sewn, and it took a long time to make. You'll have to look for good deals in order to provision your boat, but you would have done that anyway. Pirates should be thrifty, after all.

You successfully completed this step in your quest. You're worried about what Percival and Becky are up to, so you'll keep a careful eye out for them as you continue your quest and set sail to find the treasure.

This book has four different endings so if you haven't seen them all, you can:

Go back one step and ask Becky to help you

make the sail (turn to page 31).

Go back two steps and go to Fortune Fabrics

rather than Flotsam Flea Market

(turn to page 20).

Go back to the beginning and re-read the first

scene (turn to page 1).

Or if you've read all four endings,

turn to page 63.

You're back at Fortune Fabrics, and this time you're going to make a different choice and ask the pirate sewing circle to help you make the sail.

ASK THE PIRATE SEWING CIRCLE FOR HELP

You decide to ask the pirate sewing circle for help making the sail. The fabric you buy is four feet wide and 16 feet long.

Madame Dubois scowls at you as she rings up your fabric. It's a much better deal than the fabric she originally showed you, but it's still pretty expensive. If you had paid her for sewing too, you might not have had enough money for provisions.

With the pirates' help, you work out what you're going to do on a scrap of paper before marking and cutting the fabric. You will cut from the top right corner to the center of the left edge. This will make a triangle, which you will then sew onto the bottom half of the right edge.

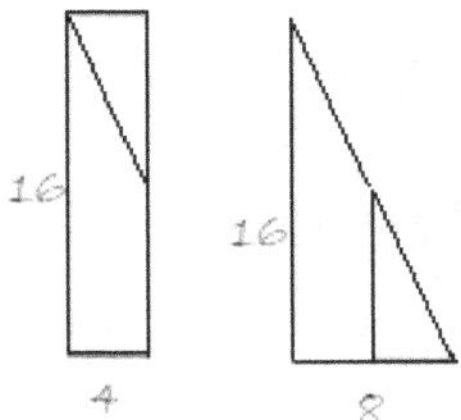

You get to work, and it goes fairly quickly. Somehow the fabric gets twisted and one of the pirates ends up sewing the wrong sides together so you have to pick out a bunch of stitches. You take a deep breath to control your frustration.

If there is any task in the world more irksome than stitch-picking, you don't know what it is.

But it all comes together in the end, and you have a really wonderful sail. You're sure it's nicer and cleaner than what you would have ended up with if you'd gotten your fabric from the flea market. You spent quite a bit on the fabric and now you spend a little more to buy the pirate sewing circle a spool of thread as a thank you. You'll have to be as thrifty as possible on the provisions, but everyone knows you should keep groups of pirates on your good side, and they helped you. You're grateful.

"Thanks, guys!" you say and head back toward the dock, your sail in your arms.

On your way to the Barnacle Bucket, you nearly bump into a girl carrying her own sail, hers a little dingy looking and stained. She clearly made it from second hand fabric.

A parrot squawks and takes off from her shoulder, and you stop and watch. You think you recognize it. Is that Pamela?

The parrot flies to a nearby boat and lands on a man's shoulder. It's Percival the Pirate! Percival doesn't seem to recognize you. "You got the sail, Becky?"

"Aye, aye, papa!" The girl calls.

She sees you looking at her and winks at you before heading up the gangplank and onto the boat.

You hurry away. *Oh, no!* you think. That sneaky pirate, Percival, and his daughter, Becky, are getting a boat ready to sail just like you are. You have a terrible suspicion that they're after the same treasure.

Your decisions here had mixed results. You spent more than you would have liked on the fabric. You'll have to look for the best deals possible in order to provision your boat, but you would have done that anyway. Pirates should be thrifty, after all. You got a good sail and successfully completed this step in your quest. You're worried about what Percival and Becky are up to, so you'll keep a careful eye out for them as you continue your quest and set sail to find the treasure.

This book has four different endings so if you haven't seen them all, you can:

Go back one step and choose to hire Madame Dubois to make the sail (turn to page 58).

Go back two steps and go to the Flotsam Flea Market rather than Fortune Fabrics (turn to page 9).

Go back to the beginning and re-read the first scene (turn to page 1).

Or if you've read all four endings, turn to page 63.

You're back at Fortune Fabrics, and this time you're going to make a different choice and hire Madame Dubois to make the sail for you.

ASK MADAME DUBOIS TO MAKE THE SAIL

You decide to hire Madame Dubois to make the sail. You're terrible at sewing, and you hate doing it. You're certain that she can get it done much faster than you can, even with the pirate sewing circle's help.

And you're right. She cuts the fabric quickly and then sews. She's so fast that you can barely see the needle! It's amazing! You and the other pirates watch in wonder. This is a sight to behold! She's done in no time. The sail looks great! But then she rings up the charge for the finished sail, and you groan. You try to haggle, offering her a lower price, but it's no good. Sadly, you open the money pouch and give it all to her.

Then, carrying the sail, you walk to Grandpa Pirate's house. You find him in the parlor. "My boy!" he says in surprise. "I didn't expect to see you today. What's wrong?"

You tell him you spent all the money Uncle Six gave you on the sail and you have nothing left for provisions.

Grandpa Pirate frowns. "That's too bad," he says. "You've failed this part of your quest. Your first task, finding Pirate Pete, tested your speed. This task tested how good you were at finding deals and saving money. A pirate has to be thrifty, you know?"

You nod and look at the floor.

"Give me that sail and your map," Grandpa Pirate says.

You do.

"I'll keep these safe for you," he says and squeezes your shoulder. "I think you're not quite ready to be a pirate captain yet, but you can try again next year."

"Thank you, Grandpa Pirate," you say. You have to wait a whole year, but at least you get a second chance.

Your decisions here didn't work out very well. You spent all the money you had. You have nothing left for provisions, so you can't set sail in search of the treasure. You have to wait a whole year to try again.

This book has four different endings so if you haven't seen them all, you can:

Go back one step and choose to ask the pirate sewing circle to help make the sail (turn to page 51).
Go back two steps and go to the Flotsam Flea Market rather than Fortune Fabrics (turn to page 9).
Go back to the beginning and re-read the first scene (turn to page 1).
Or if you've read all four endings,
turn to page 63.

CONGRATULATIONS!

You've completed the second task in your quest for the Pickled Pearl! Whether your final ending was a complete success or required you to wait a year, you are now ready to move on to the next task: *Math Pirates: Pirate Provisions.*

Or, if you would like to read all the stories about the quest for the Pickled Pearl in one book, they are in *Math Pirates: The Complete Quest for the Pickled Pearl.*

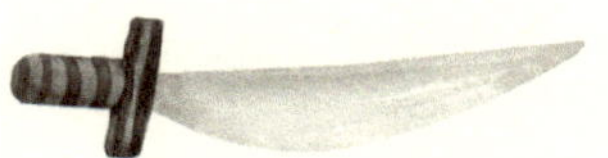

GET FREE BOOKS!

When you sign up for our mailing list at littlebooksofBIGchoices.com, you will receive the first book of every series we write for free. Head on over and sign up today!

littlebooksofBIGchoices.com

ABOUT THE AUTHOR

Once upon a time there were two little girls named Margaret.

One of the Margarets had brown hair and the other had red, and they were both poor and lived on farms, because in those days most little girls were poor and lived on farms.

And when the Margarets got older, they went to college, even though poor girls rarely did, but the Margarets were stubborn and lucky, so they got to go.

Brown-Haired Margaret became a nurse and then a librarian. Red-Haired-Margaret became a school teacher. They spent their lives helping, teaching, and reading.

Who did they help, teach, and read to the most?

Their children, of course.

Brown-Haired-Margaret had a son and Red-Haired-Margaret had a daughter, and that son and that daughter met and fell in love, and together they spent their lives reading, which is almost a happy ending…

But not quite, because what made the story even better, was that the son and the daughter had a daughter of their own and they raised her in libraries and in bookstores and left her to her own devices to play and to wander among the stacks of books, where she found innumerable adventures waiting for her between the pages.

The brown-haired Margaret and the red-haired Margaret both became white-haired-Margarets and they continued to help, and teach, and read.

And who did they help, teach, and read

to the most?

Their granddaughter, of course!

She grew up to love books EVEN MORE, than her parents had. She loved books so much, in fact, that she wanted to make more of them, and because she was stubborn and lucky, she did.

S.E. Burr's greatest desire is to spend her life helping, teaching, and reading like her grandmothers did.